The Quisine Cookbook

Introduction by Chris Kelly

FOURTH ESTATE ● *London*

First published in Great Britain in 1997 by
Fourth Estate Limited
6 Salem Road
London W2 4BU

1 3 5 7 9 10 8 6 4 2

A catalogue record for this book is available from
the British Library.

ISBN 1-85702-635-7

Home economist: Virginia Alcock
Food photography: Clive Streeter
Text design: Eric Drewery

Typeset by MATS, Southend-on-Sea, Essex

Printed in Great Britain by

The Bath Press

Contents

Illustrations

1. Spicy pork stuffed with olives, prunes and anchovies, cooked in stout and served with olive-oil mash.

2. Gâteau of roast vegetables and parma ham with goat's cheese.
   Salmon roulade with stir-fried vegetables and hollandaise sauce.

3. Squid ragout on wet polenta.
   Breast of duck served with shallot mash, beetroot purée and port and crème de cassis sauce.

4. Chicken chow mein.
   Seared peppered tuna sashimi with seaweed, served with spicy lentil salad and soy sauce.

5. Toad in the hole with rich onion gravy.

6. Hungarian pork goulash with sage dumplings.

7. Tipsy trifle of raspberries and bilberries with crème caprice.

8. Apple strudel.

9. Brandy snaps with brandy cream and caramel sauce.
   Crème brûlée with Cointreau and raspberries.

10. Croquenbouche 'French wedding cake'.

Introduction

People often ask me why food is such a big item on television. To tell you the truth, I'm always surprised that they're surprised. After all, there isn't a single important area of our lives that isn't affected by what we eat.

It goes without saying that our diet has a fundamental bearing on our health, our fitness, the way we feel and the way we perform, professionally and socially.

Equally self-evident is the link between food and money, from the family budget to the gross national product. Feeding ourselves and selling any surplus is huge business. Acquiring foodstuffs for domestic consumption and commercial gain has changed the course of history.

But food also relates to sex (who can ever forget the famous eating scene in *Tom Jones*?), art (pity the poor still-life painter deprived of fruit, game, fish, bread, etc.), fashion (whatever happened to nouvelle cuisine?), therapy (even if, like me, you're not an inspired cook, it's absorbing enough to take your mind off the overdraft), travel (making us more adventurous and demanding) and science (the label on the average tinned or chilled supermarket product can sound like a nuclear cocktail). Not to mention religion, ritual and relationships . . . Who knows how much damage has been done to our society by the increasing reluctance of families to eat together?

All human life is there, so why on earth wouldn't television want to reflect it in all its glorious variety? Hence there are documentaries, factually based magazine programmes, solo chefs vying with each other to cook in the most unlikely places, dramas set in kitchens, cooking challenges (there's hardly an institution in the land – from Trappist monastery to maximum security prison – that hasn't had a visit from a telly chef charged with feeding the inmates on a pittance) and good old-fashioned cooking without gimmicks.

So where does *Quisine* fit and what makes it different? As the title implies, it's a unique blend of quiz and cuisine, where many of the questions connect not just with some half-forgotten facts but with what's actually happening on the screen. Thus the teams have to demonstrate their powers of observation as well as their food knowledge and appreciation, identifying often relatively unusual ingredients (never easy at the best of times, but even trickier in a tense studio, in front of a live audience and against the clock).

Our guest chefs work under great pressure too. In every programme we ask the chef of the day to create two major dishes, as well as a smaller item featuring a handy short cut or crafty tip. Watching the skilful ease with which they convert literally dozens of ingredients into meals fit for a Michelin star is, for me, one of the great pleasures of the show. No wonder chefs are to the nineties what photographers were to the sixties. These are gifted craftsmen and women who are able to cook and entertain simultaneously. Try it in your own kitchen some time. Believe me, it's very, very difficult.

So that's *Quisine*. It's practical, visual, competitive, full of mouthwatering ideas and, above all, good fun. Apart from the competitive bit (cooking's demanding enough without having to worry about beating your opponent), I hope you'll find all those qualities in this book. The recipes that follow are some of *Quisine*'s greatest hits – a rich variety of dishes that taste as good as they look, don't cost an arm and a leg and don't take long to prepare.

There's nothing more satisfying than cooking for friends, provided that you get it right. With the help of this *Quisine* cookbook, you can guarantee a winner every time.

Chris Kelly

Snacks and Starters

Cheese straws

MAKES 24

100g (4oz) frozen or chilled puff pastry
50g (2oz) Parmesan cheese, grated
one beaten egg with 2 tablespoons (30ml) milk for eggwash

pinch of cayenne pepper
selection of dips to serve

Roll the pastry out on a lightly floured work surface to a 40 × 15cm (16 × 6in) rectangle, then sprinkle with the cheese and cayenne pepper. Fold the pastry over several times so the cheese and cayenne are sealed in.

Roll the pastry out so it is 3mm (⅛in) thick, then cut out 6 circles 4cm (2in) in diameter. With a smaller cutter remove the centre, leaving a circle 5mm (¼in) wide. Cut the remaining pastry into 24 strips 8 × 1cm (3 × ½in) and twist each one twice.

Place the cheese straws and circles on a lightly greased baking tray and brush with the eggwash. Bake in a pre-heated oven at 230°C (450°F/Gas Mark 8) for approximately 10 minutes, until golden brown. Cool on a wire rack.

To serve, place a bundle of straws in each circle and serve with dips.

Chef's Tip

> **How to make instant garlic toast**
> To make delicious garlic bread without the fuss and expense, toast some thick slices of bread, rub a clove of garlic, cut in half, generously over the toast, sprinkle with some freshly chopped herbs, salt and black pepper and drizzle over lots of olive oil. Very easy and very tasty.
>
> LW

Three dips with Parmesan crisps

Aubergine and yoghurt dip
2 aubergines, charred and cooked
  until soft
3 tablespoons extra virgin olive oil
2 onions, finely chopped
3 cloves garlic, finely chopped
2 teaspoons grated ginger
2 teaspoons grated coriander
1 teaspoon cumin
½ teaspoon chilli powder
1 teaspoon caster sugar
½ teaspoon salt
275ml (9fl oz) Greek yoghurt

Remove the ends, then cut the aubergines down the middle and remove the pulp with a spoon. Mash in a bowl with a fork. Heat the oil in a pan and fry the onion, garlic and ginger with the coriander, cumin, chilli, sugar, salt and aubergine for about 8 minutes, until caramelised. Add this purée to the yoghurt and mix well, then chill in a small serving bowl.

Minted pesto dip
8 cloves garlic
2 shallots
3 tablespoons fresh basil, chopped
3 tablespoons fresh coriander
4 tablespoons fresh mint
100g (4oz) roasted cashew nuts
250ml (8fl oz) extra virgin olive oil
1 teaspoon chilli sauce
½ teaspoon salt
100g (4oz) grated Parmesan cheese

In a food processor with the chopping blade in place, mince the garlic and shallots. Add the herbs and nuts and blend until finely minced, then pour in the olive oil, chilli sauce, salt and Parmesan. Mix well. Transfer the minted pesto to a small serving bowl and chill.

Green coriander, coconut and goat's cheese dip
100g (4oz) creamed coconut
75g (3oz) fresh coriander
3 green chillies, chopped
2 cloves garlic, chopped
1 lime
½ teaspoon ground cumin
½ teaspoon fresh ginger, grated
Salt to taste
100g (4oz) soft goat's cheese

In a food processor with the chopping blade in place, mix all the ingredients apart from the goat's cheese. Once blended to a fine paste, transfer to a bowl and mash in the cheese. Chill.

Parmesan crisps
100g (4oz) Parmesan cheese, grated

To prepare the Parmesan crisps, heat a frying pan and put about 1 tablespoon of the grated Parmesan cheese in the centre in a lozenge shape. Leave it to melt. Push the edges into the cheese and with a palette knife turn over and cook the other side. Serve with the three dips.

Note: The Parmesan cheese must be high quality, from a delicatessen. Otherwise, use a mature, medium-fat Italian hard cheese such as Fontina or Pecorino Romano.

*B*ouillabaisse

SERVES 4

150ml (¼ pint) virgin olive oil
2 large onions, sliced
1 bulb fennel, sliced
4 potatoes, peeled and thinly sliced
2 tomatoes, chopped
1 piece orange peel
6 filaments saffron, dissolved in 2 tablespoons hot water
4 cloves garlic, crushed
1 bay leaf
Pinch of cayenne pepper
8 crayfish, cooked
2.25 litres (4 pints) fish stock

Salt and freshly ground black pepper
2 medium whiting, cleaned, heads removed and each cut into 4 pieces
1 John Dory, cleaned, scaled, head removed and cut into 4 pieces
450g (1lb) monkfish fillet, cleaned and cut into 5cm (2in) pieces
12 mussels, washed and scrubbed
Flat leaf parsley, lemon wedges, garlic bread and garlic mayonnaise to serve

In a very large saucepan heat 1 tablespoon of the oil and fry the onions, lightly browning them. Add the fennel, potatoes, tomatoes, orange peel, saffron, garlic, bay leaf and cayenne pepper. Mix together well and cook quite fast over a fierce heat.

Add the rest of the olive oil and the crayfish, then cover with boiling fish stock. Season well and cook over a high heat for 4–5 minutes.

Put the whiting, John Dory and monkfish into the pan and continue to cook for approximately 5 minutes, until done.

Add the cleaned mussels to the pan next, ensuring that they have been scrubbed and any open ones discarded. With the lid on, cook for a further 2–3 minutes.

To serve, ladle the liquid into a serving dish. On a separate dish arrange the fish, scattered with chopped parsley and lemon wedges and serve together with the warm garlic bread and bowl of aïoli (garlic mayonnaise).

Gâteau of roast vegetables and Parma ham with goat's cheese

(see photograph 2)

SERVES 4

1 small aubergine
salt
Olive oil
1 medium courgette
1 fat roasted red pepper
Malden salt and freshly ground black
  pepper
1 lemon

4 sun-dried tomatoes
2 very ripe plum tomatoes, quartered
½ teaspoon balsamic vinegar
4 slices Parma ham
25g (1oz) rocket leaves
25g (1oz) Parmesan shavings
50g (2oz) goat's cheese

Top and tail the aubergine and cut into 8 discs. Place on a tray, lightly salt and leave for 10 minutes. Wash off the salt, drain and fry in a hot pan with olive oil until golden. Transfer to a bowl.

Cut the courgette across at an angle of 45 degrees, slicing it into 8 pieces.

Remove the skin and stalk from the roasted pepper and roughly cut into pieces. Add to the aubergines and mix.

Heat some olive oil in a frying pan and fry the courgettes, adding Malden salt, black pepper and some lemon juice. Fry until golden brown on just one side.

Add the sun-dried tomatoes, left whole, and courgettes to the aubergine mixture, cover and leave for a few hours.

Make the dressing by putting the plum tomatoes in a food processor with some olive oil, a splash of balsamic vinegar and seasoning, and liquidising until 'pulpy'. Pass through a sieve to remove the seeds.

To assemble gâteau, place a couple of slices of courgette on the base of a plate, top with a slice of aubergine, some sun-dried tomato, the pepper and another slice of aubergine. Repeat this to make 4 servings. Chill.

Take a slice of Parma ham, place some rocket leaves on top, sprinkle over some Parmesan shavings and finally the crumbled goat's cheese. Carefully roll up. Repeat this to make 4 rolls.

To serve, spoon the tomato vinaigrette around the gâteau, drizzling olive oil on top of this with some balsamic vinegar to make a dappled effect. Place the Parma ham roll on top of the gâteau with 2 leaves of rocket. Serve with a glass of red wine.

Chef's Tip

How to skin a pepper
The easy way to remove the skin from a pepper is to hold the pepper on a fork over a gas flame until it is completely charred all over. Allow to cool and the skin will easily peel off.

BT

Caesar salad

SERVES 4

50g (2oz) bread
175ml (6fl oz) extra virgin olive oil
Salt
Ground black pepper
50g (2oz) tin anchovy fillets, drained
50g (2oz) Parmesan cheese

1 egg (boiled for 1 minute)
Juice of ½ lemon
1 teaspoon English mustard
½ teaspoon Worcestershire sauce
2 cloves garlic, chopped
2 heads cos lettuce

To make the croûtons, slice the bread, remove the crusts and cut into cubes. Drizzle over olive oil and season with salt and freshly ground black pepper. Bake on a baking sheet in a pre-heated oven at 150°C (300°F/Gas Mark 2) for 15 minutes.

In a food processor make the dressing by mixing together the anchovy fillets, Parmesan cheese, boiled egg (removed from the shell), lemon juice, mustard, Worcestershire sauce, garlic and pepper. Add some olive oil, while the processor is on, to make a creamy emulsion.

Rip up the lettuce leaves (do not cut them as this makes them go brown!) and toss with the creamy dressing in a large salad bowl. Grate some Parmesan cheese on top and then scatter the croûtons.

Serve as a light lunch or early supper.

Chef's Tip

How to make a quick salad dressing
Using an empty jam jar, mix together 2 tablespoons of white wine vinegar, 8 tablespoons of olive oil, a splash of water, some crushed garlic, fresh herbs, salt and freshly ground black pepper. With the lid on the jar, shake well. Instant dressing!

LW

Samosas

SERVES 4

Pastry
100g (4oz) vegetable ghee fat, chilled
  and diced
225g (8oz) strong plain flour
Chilled water
Pinch salt

Potato filling
25g (1oz) unsalted butter
25g (1oz) onion, finely chopped
2 garlic cloves, crushed
10g (½oz) fresh ginger, finely
  chopped

½ teaspoon black mustard seeds
½ teaspoon fennel seeds
Cumin
Pinch turmeric
100g (4oz) potatoes, peeled, cooked
  and cut into 6mm (¼in) pieces
40g (1½oz) frozen peas
Pinch chilli powder
Pinch garam masala
Salt and freshly ground black pepper
Fresh coriander leaves and chutney
  to serve

Make the pastry by rubbing the vegetable ghee fat into the flour and salt, then mixing in enough water to form a dough. Cover with cling film and chill until needed.

To prepare the filling, melt the butter in a pan and soften the onion. Add the garlic, ginger, mustard seeds, fennel seeds, cumin and turmeric for colour. Add the potato, frozen peas, chilli powder, garam masala, salt and a few turns of pepper. Continue to cook for a few minutes. Remove the pastry from the fridge, take a small piece of the dough and roll it out into a circle about 12mm (½in) thick. Using a scone cutter, cut out a circle about 9cm (3½in) diameter. Cut the circle in half and brush water along the longest edge, pulling together to form a cone. Put 1 teaspoon of the filling in the cone and seal the edges together with a little water. Using a fork, nip the edges together. Repeat this process until all the pastry and filling are used.

Deep-fry the samosas in oil pre-heated to 180°C (350°F) until golden brown (approximately 5–10 minutes) and 'puffed up'. Remove from the deep-fat fryer and drain. To serve, sprinkle over roughly chopped fresh coriander and provide a chutney of your choice.

Dolmades (stuffed vine leaves)

SERVES 4

Olive oil to fry
50g (2oz) onion, finely chopped
1 clove garlic, crushed
100g (4oz) brown rice
25g (1oz) tomato purée
150ml (¼ pint) vegetable stock
25g (1oz) pine kernels
Pinch sugar
25g (1oz) currants
Juice of ½ lemon

Fresh chopped mint (optional) and
  sprigs of mint to serve
8 vine leaves
Salt and freshly ground black pepper

Avgolemeno sauce
2 egg yolks
Juice of ½ lemon
570ml (1 pint) vegetable stock

Heat some oil and sweat the onion and garlic (they should soften but not colour).

Add the brown rice and tomato purée and stir, then add the stock, pine kernels, sugar, currants, lemon juice and chopped mint. Simmer until half cooked and thickened.

Blanch the vine leaves in boiling salted water for a minute, then drain. Stuff them with a little of the rice mixture, folding in each side to form a parcel with all the ends closed. Place the stuffed leaves in an ovenproof dish, cover with 150ml (¼ pint) of water and season. Cover with aluminium foil.

Cook the vine leaves in a pre-heated oven at 180°C (350°F/Gas Mark 4) for 35–40 minutes, until tender.

Meanwhile, prepare the sauce by heating the egg yolks and lemon juice in a bain-marie until golden in colour, then gradually add some stock. Be careful not to curdle the sauce by overheating. Return to a pan and cook gently over a low heat until thickened, stirring all the time. Season to taste.

To serve the dolmades, place 2 parcels on each plate and pour over some sauce. Garnish with a sprig of fresh mint.

Blinis with soured cream and caviare

SERVES 4

(Makes 12 large blinis)
25g (1oz) melted butter
725ml (1¼ pints) milk
40g (1½oz) fresh yeast
2 teaspoons sugar
2 large eggs, separated

100g (4oz) plain flour
100g (4oz) buckwheat flour
Pinch salt
Soured cream
Caviare
Chervil to serve

Heat the butter and milk in a pan very gently until lukewarm. (Do not overheat as this will kill the yeast.)

Cream together the fresh yeast and sugar in a bowl and gradually stir in the warm milk and butter mixture and the egg yolks.

Sift the plain flour into a large mixing bowl and stir in the buckwheat flour and salt. Make a well in the centre of the flour and pour in the yeast mixture. Beat until smooth. Cover the batter and allow to rise in a warm place for approximately 45 minutes.

Whisk the egg whites until stiff and fold into the prepared batter mix.

Heat a frying pan with a little butter and drop in a generous spoonful of the blini mixture. Cook like a pancake. Keep the cooked blinis warm between sheets of greaseproof paper in a low oven.

Place the blinis on a serving plate and top each of them with a spoon of soured cream and a spoon of caviare. Garnish with chervil leaves.

Eggs Benedict

SERVES 4

3 tablespoons white wine vinegar
½ teaspoon black peppercorns, crushed
2 egg yolks
100g (4oz) unsalted clarified butter, melted
Salt and freshly ground black pepper

1 teaspoon lemon juice
4 slices Canadian or streaky bacon
2 English muffins
4 eggs
½ teaspoon paprika
1 tablespoon chopped parsley

Place 2 tablespoons of white wine vinegar in a pan with the crushed peppercorns and reduce until there is just 1 teaspoon of liquid left. Pour this into a mixing bowl.

To make hollandaise sauce, add the 2 egg yolks and whisk over a pan of simmering water until the mixture becomes light in colour. Very gradually whisk in the melted butter, taking care not to let the mixture separate. Season with salt and pepper and add the lemon juice. Cover and keep at a stable temperature, but do not overheat.

Cook the bacon on a griddle, under the grill or fry, until crisp.

Split the muffins in half and toast on each side.

Poach the eggs gently in simmering water in a pan with 1 tablespoon of white wine vinegar.

To assemble, place a slice of bacon on each toasted muffin half, lay a poached egg on top and cover with some hollandaise sauce. Sprinkle with paprika and chopped parsley and serve as a delicious brunch.

Chef's Tip

How to poach the perfect egg
To make a perfect poached egg, whisk boiling water in a pan to form a whirlpool. When this slows down slightly, drop the egg into the centre and cook until it is the consistency you like.

AT

Chicken vol-au-vents

MAKES 24 5CM (2 INCH) CASES, 12 7CM (3 INCH) CASES OR 2 15CM (6 INCH) CASES

50g (2oz) butter
50g (2oz) plain flour
275ml (½ pint) milk
Salt and freshly ground white pepper
150g (5oz) cooked chicken
50g (2oz) cooked ham
Knob of butter

50g (2oz) button mushrooms, thinly
  sliced
Pinch nutmeg
225g (8oz) puff pastry
Beaten egg for glazing
Parsley to serve

Prepare the sauce by melting 50g of butter in a pan, adding the flour and cooking gently for 1 minute, stirring all the time. Remove from the heat and gradually beat in the milk. Bring to the boil and continue to cook, still stirring, until the sauce thickens. Season to taste.

Dice the chicken and ham.

Melt the knob of butter in a pan and sweat off the mushrooms. Add the ham and chicken and toss.

Add the chicken, ham and mushrooms to the sauce and gently heat. Season with salt, pepper and nutmeg.

Roll out the pastry about 12mm (½in) thick and cut into round shapes. Place on a baking tray and brush the top of the pastry with beaten egg.

With a smaller, floured cutter, make a circular cut in each case to form an inner ring, cutting through about half the depth of the pastry.

Bake in a pre-heated oven at 220°C (425°F/Gas Mark 7) until golden brown and crisp – approximately 10 minutes.

Once baked, remove the inner circle and scoop out the soft inside while it is still warm. (Keep these centre pieces for the lids.)

Fill the cases with the hot mixture, place a top on each and arrange on a serving plate, garnished with sprigs of parsley.

Burritos

SERVES 4

8 large corn tortillas
Soured cream and Monterey Jack
   cheese to serve

Chicken filling
1 × 900g (2lb) chicken
1 onion, chopped
570ml (1 pint) chicken stock
Large pinch oregano
Salt and black pepper

Guacamole
1 ripe avocado
Juice of ½ lime
2 plum tomatoes, peeled, seeded and
   roughly chopped

2 chilli peppers, chopped
1 clove garlic, chopped
½ red onion, finely diced
½ teaspoon ground coriander
½ teaspoon ground cumin
1 tablespoon fresh coriander

Refried beans
450g (1lb) pinto beans, soaked
   overnight or canned
2 medium onions, chopped
3 tablespoons sunflower oil
½ teaspoon ground cumin
½ teaspoon ground mild chilli
   powder

To make the filling, place the chicken and chopped onion in a pan and cover with the chicken stock. Add the large pinch of oregano, salt and pepper. Bring to the boil, then simmer on a very low heat for about 75 minutes, until cooked all the way through.

Once the chicken is cooked, allow to cool, then remove from the pan and pull it apart, dicing the meat. Place in a bowl and season with salt and pepper.

Prepare the guacamole by removing the skin and stone from the avocado, and mashing the flesh in a mixing bowl with the lime juice.

Add the tomatoes, chillies, garlic, diced red onion, ground coriander, cumin and fresh coriander and mix, keeping it quite 'chunky'. Leave to chill.

For the refried beans, take the pinto beans, which have been soaked overnight, been boiled and stood covered for 1 hour (or are from a can) and mash to a coarse, chunky consistency.

Sauté the onion in a frying pan heated with the sunflower oil, and sprinkle in the ground cumin and chilli powder. Add the mashed beans and cook over a medium heat until thickened and slightly darker in colour.

To assemble the burritos, place the chicken in the centre of 4 of the tortillas and the refried beans in the centre of the other 4. Top each with guacamole, followed by the soured cream, then roll them up.

Either serve with extra soured cream or sprinkle with grated Monterey Jack cheese and toast under a hot grill.

Chef's Tip

The best way to stone an avocado pear
Cut the avocado in half lengthways and twist the halves in opposite directions to separate. Place a sharp knife in the stone and twist to remove it. Remove the skin, brush the avocado with lemon juice to prevent browning and slice into a fan, or use as you wish.

AWT

Bubble and squeak

SERVES 4

2 leeks
50g (2oz) unsalted butter
50g (2oz) back bacon, chopped
1 tablespoon snipped fresh chives
1 clove garlic, crushed
100g (4oz) beef, cooked until rare
  and chopped

350g (12oz) cooked potatoes,
  mashed
100g (4oz) cooked green cabbage,
  finely chopped
Salt and freshly ground black pepper
Sunflower oil for shallow-frying
4 eggs (size 1)

Cut off the ends of the leeks and slice.

Melt the butter in a frying pan and add the leeks and bacon, the chives, garlic and the cut-up beef. Cook for about 5 minutes, until browned.

Fold the bacon mixture into the mashed potato and add the cabbage and some salt and black pepper.

Divide the mixture into 4 equal-sized balls and shape each into a cake. Fry the cakes in hot oil in a large frying pan for approximately 5 minutes, browning both sides.

Shallow-fry the eggs and place on top of each cake of bubble and squeak.

Chef's Tip

How to make cappuccino in a cafetiere
Heat some full-fat or semi-skimmed milk (this does not work with skimmed milk) until just below boiling point. Put some hot coffee in a cup. Pour the hot milk into a cafetiere and carefully push the top up and down to create lots of froth. Add this frothy milk to the coffee and sprinkle the top with ground chocolate or coffee. Hey presto, a delicious cappuccino!

AWT

Vegetarian Dishes

Mozzarella and tomato soufflé

SERVES 4

50g (2oz) butter
25g (1oz) plain flour
150ml (¼ pint) milk
½ tablespoon English mustard powder
25g (1oz) onion, finely chopped
1 clove garlic, crushed

4 large tomatoes, skinned, deseeded and diced
75g (3oz) mozzarella cheese, finely diced
Salt and freshly ground black pepper
3 eggs (size 3), separated
Extra butter for greasing the ramekin dishes

Melt 25g (1oz) butter with the flour and cook for 2 minutes, being careful not to let the mixture colour.

Slowly stir in the milk to form a smooth, thick sauce and cook for about 4 minutes. Season with the mustard powder. Remove from heat.

Meanwhile, melt the remaining butter in a pan and add the onion, garlic and tomatoes and cook for 2 minutes. Remove from heat.

Mix into the white sauce the mozzarella, salt and black pepper. Add the egg yolks and stir thoroughly.

Add the tomato mixture to the white sauce.

Whisk the egg whites to form stiff peaks and then very gently fold into the mixture.

Pour the mixture into 4 well-greased individual soufflé moulds and bake in a pre-heated oven at 190°C (375°F/Gas Mark 5) for 25–30 minutes.

Serve and eat immediately once cooked.

Aubergine and tomato croûte with spinach, sorrel and rocket salad

SERVES 4

2 medium aubergines
1 slice brown bread
3 cloves garlic
1 tablespoon chopped parsley
Juice of ½ lemon
7 tablespoons olive oil
Salt and freshly ground black pepper
1 small granary French stick
Extra virgin olive oil
450g (1lb) ripe plum tomatoes,
   roughly chopped

1 tablespoon balsamic vinegar
1½ tablespoons chopped fresh basil

Spinach, sorrel and rocket salad
100g (4oz) baby spinach, washed
25g (1oz) sorrel, washed and roughly
   shredded
50g (2oz) rocket, washed
2 tablespoons olive oil
Juice of 1 lemon
1 clove garlic, crushed

Prick the aubergines with a fork and bake in a pre-heated oven at 200°C (400°F/Gas Mark 6) on a lightly oiled baking sheet for 35 minutes. Cut in half lengthways and scoop out the flesh.

Dip the slice of bread into water, then squeeze out.

In a food processor purée the aubergine with the bread, garlic, parsley, lemon juice and 5 tablespoons olive oil until smooth and creamy. Transfer to a bowl and season to taste with salt and black pepper.

Cut the French stick into thick slices and lightly brush with about 1 tablespoon olive oil and lay on a baking tray. Bake in the oven for about 5 minutes. Heat 1 tablespoon of olive oil in a frying pan and add the tomatoes. Toss over a high heat for 30 seconds, pour in the vinegar and add the basil. Season to taste.

Remove the croûtes from the oven and spread on to each a generous portion of the aubergine butter. Place the croûtes on a large platter, spoon the hot tomatoes over them and serve with salad leaves tossed in a dressing made by mixing the oil, lemon and garlic.

Tower of roast artichokes with celeriac purée, wild mushrooms and hollandaise sauce

SERVES 4

450g (1lb) celeriac, peeled and cubed
275ml (½ pint) double cream
Pinch nutmeg
4 large artichoke hearts
100g (4oz) mixed wild mushrooms:
   chanterelle, shitake and oyster
100g (4oz) butter
Salt and freshly ground black pepper
1 clove garlic, crushed
1 fennel bulb, sliced
50g (2oz) Gruyère cheese, grated
50g (2oz) Cheddar cheese, grated

Hollandaise sauce
3 egg yolks
Splash of white wine vinegar
1 tablespoon lemon juice
1 large bunch of basil, roughly
   chopped
350g (12oz) unsalted butter, melted

Stew the celeriac in a pan for approximately 20 minutes with the cream until it becomes a stiff purée. Add the nutmeg.

Boil the artichokes for approximately 20–25 minutes, according to size and freshness. Remove the outer leaves then the 'choke' from the heart, cut the hearts across into 3 slices.

Chop the wild mushrooms and sauté in 50g (2oz) butter with salt and pepper. Poach the fennel in 50g (2oz) butter and ¼ pint water for approximately 15 minutes, until soft. Then add this and the garlic to the mushrooms.

Grease some round cutter moulds and put on a baking tray. Place a round of artichoke heart in the bottom of each cutter, adding a small amount of celeriac purée and then some wild mushrooms to the mixture.

Lay another slice of artichoke heart on top and repeat the process, finishing with a slice of artichoke. Sprinkle with the mixed cheese and season.

Bake in a pre-heated oven at 190°C (375°F/Gas Mark 5) for approximately 20 minutes.

Make the hollandaise sauce by mixing the eggs yolks, vinegar, lemon juice and basil in a food processor and slowly adding the melted warm butter.

Once the artichoke towers are cooked, take the moulds away, place a tower on a plate and top with the hollandaise sauce.

Chef's Tip

How to skin and chop a tomato

If you want to have chef's-style fresh tomato pieces, easy. There is no need to put the tomatoes in boiling water or over a flame. Simply cut them into quarters and remove the seeds. Then using a sharp knife slice off the skin and finely dice the flesh. Ideal for scattering on your salad.

BT

Moroccan nut koftas with pecan nuts and hazelnuts, served on a bed of brown rice with a yoghurt tartar sauce

SERVES 4

200g (7oz) pecan nuts
200g (7oz) hazelnuts
2 tablespoons walnut oil
1 teaspoon cinnamon
1 teaspoon mace
1 teaspoon ground ginger
Pinch nutmeg
2 eggs, beaten
6 tablespoons fresh breadcrumbs
Salt and freshly ground black pepper
Sunflower oil for frying
50g (2oz) dried apricots, chopped
50g (2oz) sultanas

225g (8oz) brown rice, cooked

Yoghurt tartar sauce
350g (12oz) Greek yoghurt
75g (3oz) gherkins, finely chopped
75g (3oz) shallots, finely chopped
50g (2oz) capers, chopped
Juice and rind 1 lime
1 green chilli, seeded and finely diced
1 tablespoon chopped parsley
1 teaspoon mustard powder
55ml (2fl oz) olive oil
Flat-leaf parsley to serve

Pre-heat the oven to 200°C (400°F/Gas Mark 6). Place the nuts on a baking tray and roast until toasted (approximately 10 minutes). Cool and place the nuts in a processor and coarsely grind, adding the walnut oil, cinnamon, mace, ginger and nutmeg. Process until combined.

Transfer to a bowl and beat in the eggs, then fold in the breadcrumbs. Season with salt and pepper and form the mixture into small cakes. Heat some sunflower oil in a pan and fry the koftas on each side until golden brown. In another frying pan, lightly fry the chopped apricots and sultanas in more sunflower oil then add the rice. Heat through. Prepare the tartar sauce by mixing all the ingredients together, adding the olive oil gradually, beating all the time. To serve arrange the koftas on top of the rice, drizzle over the tartar sauce and garnish with flat-leaf parsley.

Potato gnocchi

SERVES 2 AS A MAIN COURSE OR 4 AS A SIDE DISH OR STARTER

600g (1lb 5oz) potatoes, peeled
60g (2½oz) Parmesan cheese, grated,
  plus extra for topping
2 egg yolks
60g (2½oz) plain flour
Pinch ground nutmeg
Salt and freshly ground black pepper
40g (1½oz) butter, melted

Tomato sauce
1 onion, finely chopped
1 celery stick, finely chopped
1 small leek, finely chopped
1 tablespoon olive oil
1 tablespoon tomato purée
6 plum tomatoes, roughly chopped,
  or 1 can chopped tomatoes
Splash white wine
Fresh basil, roughly chopped, plus
  sprig of basil to serve
Salt and freshly ground black pepper

Boil the potatoes in salted water until soft, then drain and leave in the pan to dry out over a low heat for a couple of minutes, shaking them to avoid burning.

Pass the potatoes through a fine sieve into a mixing bowl, then add the Parmesan cheese, egg yolks, plain flour, nutmeg, salt and pepper and mix to a smooth texture. Prepare the sauce by frying the onion, celery and leek in the olive oil until softened, then adding the tomato purée, tomatoes and wine. Simmer for about 15 minutes, then purée in a food processor. Stir in the chopped basil and season.

Put the gnocchi mixture into a piping bag with a large plain nozzle. Pipe the mixture into a saucepan containing boiling salted water, using a sharp knife to cut into little dumplings as it comes through the nozzle (do not cook too many dumplings in the pan at one time). When cooked they float to the surface.

Remove the cooked gnocchi with a slotted spoon, drain them and place in a heatproof serving dish. Sprinkle the top with some melted butter and grated Parmesan cheese and place under a hot grill to brown.

Serve with the tomato sauce and garnish with a sprig of fresh basil.

Tonnarelli with melon and ricotta cream sauce, served with tomato and basil crostini and a rocket, chicory and Parmesan salad

SERVES 4

225g (8oz) tonnarelli pasta
50g (2oz) butter
1 medium-sized cantaloupe melon
Salt and freshly ground black pepper
Juice ½ lemon
1 teaspoon tomato purée
275ml (½ pint) double cream
225g (8oz) ricotta cheese
Parmesan cheese, grated

Tomato and basil crostini
8 diagonal 6mm (¼in) slices French
   baguette, old and dry
2 tablespoons extra virgin olive oil

1 clove garlic, halved
2 tomatoes, sliced
1 tablespoon red onion, diced
Fresh basil
1 teaspoon balsamic vinegar
Maldon salt

Rocket, chicory and Parmesan salad
2 handfuls rocket, washed and dried
1 head chicory, split into leaves
Balsamic vinegar
Extra virgin olive oil
50g (2oz) Parmesan cheese shavings
4 lemon wedges

Cook the tonnarelli pasta in boiling salted water until al dente.

Prepare the sauce by melting the butter in a large pan over a medium heat.

Remove the rind and seeds from the melon and cut into small dice. Add the melon to the butter and stir so that all the pieces are coated. Cook until almost all the liquid released has evaporated.

Season generously, then add the lemon juice and tomato purée and stir. Pour in the cream and cook, stirring frequently, until it has reduced by half. Add the ricotta cheese.

Pre-heat the oven to 180°C (350°F/Gas Mark 4). Prepare the crostini by drizzling the slices of bread with olive oil and baking for about 10 minutes. Remove from oven and rub with the garlic. Top each slice with tomato, red onion, basil leaves and a pinch of salt. Drizzle over balsamic vinegar and oil.

Prepare the salad, dress with balsamic vinegar and oil and decorate with Parmesan curls and lemon wedges.

Toss the pasta into the sauce, sprinkle over some grated Parmesan cheese and serve with the crostini and salad.

Chef's Tip

How to make vegetable ribbons
Using a potato peeler, peel some carrots, courgettes and asparagus to create long ribbon-like strands. Blanch very quickly in boiling salted water for just a few seconds, then toss with butter and fresh chopped herbs. Serve as a delicious vegetable accompaniment or mix with freshly cooked tagliatelle.

AWT

Risotto primavera

SERVES 4

100ml (4fl oz) olive oil
1 onion, finely diced
450g (1lb) Arborio rice
300ml (10fl oz) dry white wine
900ml (1½ pints) vegetable stock
50g (2oz) carrot, diced
50g (2oz) celery, diced
50g (2oz) leek, diced
50g (2oz) red pepper, diced

50g (2oz) courgette, diced
40g (1½oz) butter
Sea salt and black pepper
50g (2oz) Parmesan cheese, grated,
   plus extra to serve
2 tablespoons whipped cream
1 tablespoon chives, chopped
Fresh basil sprigs to serve

Warm the frying pan on the hob (not too hot) and add the olive oil. Gently fry the onion for 1 minute so that it softens.

Add the rice to the pan and shake it so that each grain is coated. Pour in the white wine and vegetable stock and simmer for 20 minutes to reduce. Add all the vegetables and cook for a further 10 minutes, stirring constantly.

Beat in the butter and season with plenty of ground sea salt and black pepper. Finally, stir in the freshly grated Parmesan cheese, lightly whipped cream and chopped fresh chives. Continue to cook for several minutes to thicken.

To serve, sprinkle over some Parmesan cheese and fresh basil sprigs.

*V*egetable curry with pumpkin and pilau rice

SERVES 4

900ml (1½ pints) coconut milk
1 teaspoon grated fresh ginger
½ teaspoon ground turmeric
1 stalk lemon grass, finely chopped
5cm (2in) cinnamon stick
1 onion
2 cloves garlic, finely sliced
3 green chillies, deseeded and finely chopped
1 Savoy cabbage
3 heads bok choi (Chinese cabbage)
75g (3oz) shitake mushrooms
6 new potatoes, boiled and halved
75g (3oz) okra
6 patty pan squashes, quartered
225g (8oz) pumpkin

2 tomatoes, peeled, seeded and quartered
275ml (½ pint) coconut cream
Salt and freshly ground black pepper
Fresh coriander, roughly chopped, to serve

Pilau rice
25g (1oz) butter
225g (8oz) long-grain rice (white)
600ml (1 pint) vegetable stock
1 onion, diced
25g (1oz) raisins
1 cardamom pod
25g (1oz) flaked almonds

Prepare the pilau rice by melting the butter in a pan, adding the rice and gently frying for about 5 minutes, constantly stirring. Add the stock, transfer the mixture to an ovenproof dish, cover and cook in a pre-heated oven at 180°C (350°F/Gas Mark 4) for about 35 minutes.

Prepare the curry by pouring the coconut milk into a large saucepan on the heat and adding the ginger, turmeric, lemon grass and cinnamon stick. Bring to the boil.

Shred the onion and add to the saucepan with the garlic and chillies and cook for 15 minutes.

Shred the cabbage and bok choi and quarter the mushrooms.

Add all the vegetables, one at a time, depending on how long each takes to cook (potatoes, okra, patty pan squash, pumpkin, tomatoes, cabbage, bok choi and finally the shitake mushrooms).

Once cooked, add the coconut cream and salt and pepper to taste and simmer for a further 5 minutes.

Cook the flavouring for the pilau rice by frying the onion, raisins, cardamom pod and almonds until browned. Mix in with the cooked rice.

To serve, dish the rice on to dinner plates, spoon over some of the curry and sprinkle with the coriander. Warmed naan bread and a cool beer make perfect accompaniments.

Chef's Tip

How to make the perfect roux sauce

To make the perfect roux sauce, use equal quantities of butter and flour. For 570ml (1 pint) of sauce, melt 25g (1oz) butter in a pan, then stir in 25g (1oz) flour and cook gently over the heat, stirring (do not colour for a white sauce). Add 570ml (1 pint) of hot milk and cook for about 5 minutes, stirring continuously, until thick and smooth. If the sauce is lumpy, pass through a sieve using the back of a wooden spoon, so the lumps remain in the sieve and not in the sauce!

NN

Seafood and Fish

Noodle paella

SERVES 4

4 tablespoons olive oil
1 large onion, chopped
6 small chicken joints
Salt and freshly ground black pepper
2 plum tomatoes, chopped
450g (1lb) dried macaroni
2 pinches saffron powder
Sprig rosemary
225g (8oz) flat beans, cut into 5cm (2in) pieces

1 bay leaf
2 cloves garlic, crushed
1.2 litres (2 pints) fish stock
150ml (¼ pint) white wine
12 raw tiger prawns
12 slices garlic sausage
12 mussels, soaked, scrubbed and cleaned
2 lemons, cut into thick wedges

Heat the oil in a paella pan and fry the onion until softened and coloured. Season the chicken joints with salt and black pepper and fry gently in the same pan, turning to ensure the chicken cooks evenly.

Add to the pan the tomatoes, macaroni, saffron, rosemary, flat beans, bay leaf, garlic, stock and wine. Season well and cook over a medium heat for approximately 20 minutes, adding extra stock if necessary. Prepare the tiger prawns by cutting them down the shell and removing any black intestines.

Add to the pan the prawns, sausage and all closed, scrubbed mussels (do not cook any mussels which have not closed after soaking). Cook for 4–5 minutes and season to taste. (Discard any mussels that have not opened during cooking.) Serve the paella with the lemon wedges, crusty bread and a glass of red wine.

Cajun seafood gumbo with red snapper and prawns, chorizo sausage and okra, served with rice

SERVES 4

125ml (4fl oz) oil
60g (2½oz) plain flour
1½ litres (2½ pints) fish stock
2 tablespoons Cajun seasoning
1 × 250g (9oz) red snapper
250g (9oz) king prawns
150g (5oz) celery, chopped
150g (5oz) white onion, chopped
2 cloves garlic, chopped

A little oil for frying
1 small chorizo sausage, sliced thickly
150g (5oz) okra, chopped
225g (8oz) white rice
Pinch saffron
50g (2oz) flaked almonds, toasted
2 limes, sliced, to serve
Fresh chervil to serve

Make the roux for the gumbo by heating the oil in a pan and slowly stirring in the flour. Keep the heat high and stir continuously (take care as the oil becomes hot). The roux will stick, so keep scraping the bottom of the pan. Cook for 10–15 minutes, then take off the heat and stir until cooled.

Bring the stock to the boil, add the roux gradually with 1 tablespoon of Cajun seasoning and simmer for about an hour.

Cut the red snapper into pieces and peel the prawns, removing any intestines.

Fry the celery, onion and garlic and add the sausage and fish.

Add the fish mix and okra to the sauce, with 1 tablespoon more of the Cajun seasoning. Simmer for 45 minutes over a very low heat.

Cook the rice in boiling salted water until al dente and drain. Add the saffron mixed with water and stir in the almonds.

Once the gumbo is cooked, serve on a bed of rice and garnish with fresh chervil and slices of lime.

Warm pasta salad of taglianini with aubergine and peppers

SERVES 4

3 aubergines
125ml (5fl oz) olive oil for marinating
75ml (3fl oz) soy sauce
75ml (3fl oz) Japanese rice vinegar
450g (1lb) taglianini
2 tablespoons olive oil for frying
2 chicken breasts, diced (12mm/½in)
3 red peppers, roasted and peeled
3 tablespoons freshly squeezed lime juice
2 tablespoons brown sugar
2 tablespoons fish sauce (nam pla)

1 teaspoon chilli sauce
2 tablespoons spring onion, finely chopped
3 tablespoons chopped fresh coriander, plus extra to serve
3 tablespoons chopped mint, plus extra to serve
2 tablespoons minced fresh ginger
2 cloves garlic, crushed
12 raw, shelled prawns
Freshly ground black pepper

Trim the ends of the aubergines and cut each lengthways into 6 pieces. Marinate in a bowl with 3fl oz olive oil, the soy sauce and rice vinegar for about an hour (turn them every 15 minutes).

Cook the taglianini until al dente. Heat 2 tablespoons olive oil in a frying pan and add the chicken, turning occasionally.

Put the marinated aubergines on a chargrill and cook for about 4 minutes on each side, until brown and softened. Once cooked, dice.

Remove the seeds from the roasted peppers and dice the flesh. Mix the aubergine, pepper, lime juice, brown sugar, fish sauce, chilli sauce, spring onion, coriander, mint, ginger and garlic and the remaining 2fl oz oil. Turn the chicken in the frying pan and add the peeled prawns, cooking for a few minutes. Add the aubergine and pepper salsa and season just with black pepper.

Pour the chicken, prawn and salsa on the pasta and toss. Serve with warm bruschetta and sprinkle with fresh coriander and mint.

Marinated roast langoustines with crispy vegetables

SERVES 4

Marinade
1 tablespoon fish sauce
1 tablespoon light soy sauce
1 red chilli, deseeded and finely
  chopped
½ teaspoon chilli oil
Juice and zest 1 lime
Salt and freshly ground black pepper

For the langoustines and vegetables
10 large langoustines
1 medium carrot
1 medium courgette
Sunflower oil
Lime juice
Fresh dill, chopped
Garlic bread to serve

Make the marinade in a mixing bowl by mixing all the ingredients together.

Prepare the langoustines by tearing them in half, removing the tails. Lay the tails belly down on a chopping board and, with a sharp knife, cut them in half along their length, removing any veins. Place the halves shell-side down on a tray and sprinkle over half the marinade. Leave for 1 hour.

Meanwhile, prepare the vegetables. Peel the carrot and courgette to remove the outer layer. Then, using a potato peeler, cut as many long, thin slices from both of them as you can.

Deep-fry in sunflower oil heated to 180°C (350°F) for approximately 2–3 minutes. (NB. Put the carrots in first as they take slightly longer.) Drain on kitchen paper. Heat some sunflower oil in a large frying pan and fry the langoustines, skin-side down, adding extra oil if necessary and some lime juice.

To serve, arrange 5 of the langoustine halves on each plate, flesh-side up and tails pointing to the centre of the plate. Sprinkle over some of the crispy vegetables and drizzle with the remaining marinade.

Sprinkle over the fresh dill and serve with hot garlic bread.

Squid ragout on wet polenta

(see photograph 3)

SERVES 4

450g (1lb) small squid, cleaned
1 red pepper, halved, deseeded and
  sliced
1 orange pepper, halved, deseeded
  and sliced
1 fennel bulb, thinly sliced
2 tablespoons virgin olive oil
1 bunch spring onions, chopped
1 clove garlic, crushed
12 Greek black olives, pitted
4 cardamom pods, crushed
1 red chilli, deseeded and finely
  chopped
150ml (½ pint) white wine

1 × 400g (14oz) can cherry tomatoes
1 tablespoon small capers
Salt and finely ground black pepper

Wet polenta
225g (8oz) instant 'quick cook'
  polenta
900ml (1½ pints) vegetable stock
150ml (¼ pint) white wine
Salt and freshly ground black pepper
2 tablespoons virgin olive oil
2 tablespoons flat-leaf parsley,
  roughly chopped

Cut the clean squid bodies open, pull out the backbone and, using a small sharp knife, slash gently into the flesh in a lattice fashion, taking care not to cut too deeply.

Fry the peppers and fennel in oil until softened. Add the squid and stir-fry over a fierce heat for 1 minute.

Add the spring onions, garlic, olives, cardamoms, chilli, white wine, cherry tomatoes and capers and cook for about 20 minutes.

Cook the instant polenta in the vegetable stock and white wine, stirring continually until cooked. Once cooked, season well and serve on a large serving platter. Drizzle over the olive oil and scatter with parsley.

Season the squid ragout and spoon over the polenta.

Serve with a crisp green salad and chilled white wine.

Kebabs of cockles and mussels with herb and almond butter

SERVES 4

25 cockles
25 fat mussels
8 large spring onions
100g (4oz) butter, softened
1 teaspoon almonds, chopped
1 teaspoon oatmeal

50g (2oz) white breadcrumbs
1 clove garlic, crushed
1 tablespoon chopped parsley
Salt and black pepper
4 large beef tomatoes
Olive oil

Soak the cockles and mussels for several hours, throwing away any open ones. Wash and debeard them.

Steam them in a pan of water with the lid on until opened. Throw away any unopened ones. Shell them.

Cut the spring onions into 2cm (1in) pieces and thread them and the cockles and mussels alternately on a skewer.

Mix the butter with the almonds, oatmeal, breadcrumbs, garlic, parsley and seasoning and lay out on a tray.

Roll the kebabs in the mixture and cook under a hot grill, turning occasionally, until they are very hot and browned.

Serve on a bed of sliced tomatoes, sprinkled with olive oil.

Chef's Tip

How to feather a sauce
To turn a plain piece of poached fish into a fantastic dinner party dish, put the fish on a dinner plate, pour some smooth tomato sauce around it and drizzle a teaspoon of cream over the sauce. Using a cocktail stick or skewer, swirl the cream round to feather it. Garnish with a sprig of fresh herb such as dill or flat-leaf parsley on the fish.

NN

Seared peppered tuna sashimi with seaweed, served with spicy lentil salad and soy sauce

(see photograph 4)

SERVES 4

50g (2oz) finely ground black pepper mixed with ½ teaspoon powdered star anise
450g (1lb) trimmed tuna loin, in the piece
2 dessertspoons wasabi powder (Japanese green horseradish)
6 tablespoons mayonnaise

Spicy lentil salad
225g (8oz) lentils de Puy, washed
3 cloves garlic, peeled
275ml (½ pint) vegetable stock
75ml (3fl oz) extra virgin olive oil
1 red onion, peeled and finely diced

4 large red chillies, chargrilled or roasted, peeled, deseeded and mashed
Grated zest and juice 2 limes
Salt and freshly ground black pepper

Dipping sauce
1 teaspoon juices from grated fresh ginger
150ml (5fl oz) light Japanese soy sauce
½ teaspoon wasabi paste

Nori (seaweed) sheets
Fresh coriander, roughly chopped, to serve

For the Tuna Sashimi, place the black pepper mixed with the star anise in a shallow tray and roll the tuna in it, pressing the pepper into the flesh. Heat a thick-based frying pan, without fat, over a high heat. Place the tuna in the pan and sear each side until the heat has penetrated 6mm (¼in) all round.

Mix the wasabi powder to a smooth paste by gradually adding warm water in a small bowl and leave to rest for 10 minutes until thickened to a paste. Mix the paste with the mayonnaise, little by little, until the right heat is achieved. Be careful as the wasabi paste is very hot.

Cook the lentils with the garlic cloves and stock over a medium heat, then boil and simmer for 20–25 minutes. Drain into a mixing bowl once cooked. Add the oil, onion, chillies, lime zest and juice and seasoning to the lentils and mix well.

Chop the nori, after gently heating by holding over the hob, and place to one side.

Prepare the dipping sauce by mixing together the ginger juice, soy sauce and wasabi paste. Leave to stand for 30 minutes.

Cut the cold tuna into very thin slices using a simple single draw from the top to the bottom with a sharp knife.

Fill a piping bag, made from greaseproof paper with a small piece cut off the end, with wasabi mayonnaise.

To serve, place a mound of lentils in the centre of a plate, place 2 slices of the tuna against them and pipe the mayonnaise in zigzag lines over the tuna. Garnish with the nori and coriander and serve with dipping sauce.

Chef's Tip

How to dress a crab

Place a cooked crab on its back on a large chopping board. Remove the legs first by holding each firmly close to the body with one hand and twisting them off, steadying the body with the other hand. Remove the two claws in the same way. With the tail flap towards you and the head away from you, hold the shell firmly, press the body section upwards from beneath the tail flap and ease out with your thumbs until the body is detached. This will come out in one piece. Remove the inedible grey feather-like gills ('dead man's fingers') from the body section and discard them. Remove all the brown and white meat from the shell and, using a rolling pin and fork, remove all the meat from the legs and claws. Wash the shell under cold water and dry. Arrange all the white and brown meat in the shell and decorate with lemon slices.

BT

Salmon fishcakes

SERVES 4

350g (12oz) potatoes, peeled and boiled
Salt and freshly ground black pepper
1 egg, beaten
175g (6oz) cod, poached
Juice ½ lemon
1 tablespoon chopped parsley
1 tablespoon chopped dill

1 egg, hard-boiled and shelled
175g (6oz) salmon, poached
Flour for coating
2 eggs and 150ml (¼ pint) milk, beaten together, for coating
Fresh or dried breadcrumbs
Sunflower oil for frying

Cream the potatoes with salt and pepper in a bowl. Stir in the beaten egg, the cooked cod, lemon juice and herbs, mixing together well.

Roughly chop the hard-boiled egg and add to the potato mix.

Flake the salmon, leaving it in large chunks, and gently add it to the potato mix, taking care not to break up the flakes. Season to taste.

Lightly flour the work surface and turn out the mixture. Divide into 4 or 8 equal-sized cakes and pat them into round, flat shapes.

Dip each cake into a bowl of flour, followed by a bowl of beaten egg and milk mixture and then finally the breadcrumbs. Remould if necessary back into round cakes, cover and chill until required. To fry, heat some sunflower oil in a frying pan over a medium heat and cook until crispy and golden brown on both sides. Serve with a crisp salad, French fries and garlic mayonnaise.

Chef's Tip

How to make spicy French fries
Cut potatoes into thin French fries and soak them in a bowl of milk mixed with cayenne pepper, turmeric and any favourite spices for two hours (this helps the chips become crisper). Once soaked, deep-fry until crisp, then drain and sprinkle with more spices before serving.

AT

Kullenskink

SERVES 4

700g (1½lb) smoked undyed Finnan haddock fillets, skinned
600ml (1 pint) water
2 cloves
2 bay leaves
50g (2oz) unsalted butter
2 onions, finely chopped

1 teaspoon soft thyme leaves
600ml (1 pint) milk
275g (10oz) mashed potato
150ml (5fl oz) double cream
Salt and freshly ground white pepper
Fresh chives

Cook the smoked haddock in a large saucepan with the water, cloves and bay leaves by bringing it to the boil and then allowing it to simmer for 20 minutes. Leave to cool once cooked. Strain the cooking liquor, retain it and flake the smoked haddock into small pieces.

Heat the butter in a large pan on the hob and cook the onion and thyme. Pour in the fish liquor, bring to the boil and cook on a high heat for 15 minutes.

Add the milk and mashed potato to the pan and whisk until the potato is smooth. This is the base for the Kullenskink.

Fold in the smoked haddock and, once the soup is boiling, add the cream. Season with salt and white pepper and sprinkle with snipped chives. Serve with crusty bread rolls.

Chef's Tip

How to skin fresh fish fillets
The sure way to skin any fresh fillet of fish is to lay the fish skin side down on a board and, using a sharp knife, make an incision across the tail end to release the skin, then sprinkle with salt. Hold on to the skin and, with the knife between the flesh and skin, work along, pressing the flat side of the blade against the skin with an even tension so you do not press too hard and slice through it.

NN

Fettucine of monkfish and mussels with a curry and coriander velouté

SERVES 4

700g (1½lb) mussels, cleaned and debearded
100ml (4fl oz) white wine
25g (1oz) unsalted butter
2 shallots, finely diced
4 button mushrooms, finely sliced
2 teaspoons medium curry paste
175g (6oz) fettucine, cooked

2 tablespoons olive oil
225g (8oz) monkfish fillet, trimmed of all skin
Maldon salt
Fresh ground black pepper
1 lemon
175ml (6fl oz) double cream
Fresh coriander, roughly chopped

Steam open the mussels by cooking them with the white wine in a large pan with a lid. This should take about 3 minutes. Once ready, strain the rich mussel stock and reserve it.

Prepare the sauce by melting the butter in a pan on a low/medium heat. Add the shallots and cook for a few minutes, then add the mushrooms and curry paste. Stir and soften.

Drain the pasta and pick the mussels from their shells, keeping them to one side. Add a splash of white wine to the pan and reduce to get rid of the alcohol, and also stir in 6fl oz of the reserved mussel stock. Leave this cooking on a high heat to reduce.

Heat another pan on a high heat and add the olive oil. Cut the monkfish into small, thin medallions and cook on just 1 side for about 45 seconds. The monkfish should caramelise slightly, but you must not move the pieces. Season with salt, pepper and lemon juice. Add the cream to the sauce and boil. Add the pasta and the mussels.

To serve, pour the sauce with the pasta and mussels on to a large serving platter, sprinkle over the chopped coriander and put the medallions of monkfish on top.

Sausage of fresh salmon, crab and ginger, served with scrambled eggs and Madeira jus

SERVES 4

50g (2oz) butter
1 piece of root ginger, finely chopped
225g (8oz) white crab meat
1 tablespoon chopped chives or
    spring onions
¼ teaspoon cayenne pepper
Salt

1 × 275g (10oz) salmon fillet
570ml (1 pint) chicken stock
4 whole eggs
2 tablespoons double cream
1 tablespoon fresh chervil, roughly
    chopped, and extra leaves to serve
Splash of Madeira

In a saucepan melt half the butter. Add the chopped ginger and allow to sweat until tender without browning.

Add the crab meat, chives, cayenne pepper and salt to the pan, mixing well, then allow to cool.

Remove the skin from the salmon fillet, trim to make into a square, then slice from right to left into 4 thin slices.

Place each salmon slice on a piece of cling film and top with the crab mixture down the centre. Roll up tightly to form sausages and secure the ends by twisting them. Place in a steamer for 3–4 minutes. Add a splash of Madeira to thin it down and flavour it.

In a pan, heat the chicken stock briskly and reduce by about half, until it thickens slightly.

In another pan, heat the remaining butter, then add the eggs and stir continuously until they are scrambled. Stir in the double cream, season and add the chopped chervil. Transfer to a warm dish.

To serve, place a spoonful of scrambled egg on each plate, remove the cling film from the sausages and place 1 on top of the egg. Pour the Madeira jus around and garnish with some chervil leaves.

Salmon roulade with stir-fried vegetables and hollandaise sauce

(see photograph 2)

SERVES 4

Salmon roulade
5 × 175g (6oz) salmon fillets
4 tablespoons double cream
100g (4oz) chopped spinach, cooked
 and cooled
Pinch nutmeg
Salt
Freshly ground black pepper

Stir-fried vegetables
25g (1oz) unsalted butter
225g (8oz) mange tout, shredded
16 new potatoes, cooked and halved
1 clove garlic, crushed

Hollandaise sauce
2 egg yolks
2 tablespoons white wine vinegar
225g (8oz) unsalted butter, melted
Salt and pepper

In a food processor, purée 1 salmon fillet and add the cream, spinach, nutmeg and seasoning.

Take the remaining salmon fillets and cut each almost in half to open it up, but not completely cutting through. Wrap each opened-out fillet in cling film and flatten with a rolling pin or the back of a knife. Season each fillet and spread the mousse filling on top. Roll up in cling film, like a Swiss roll, and tie at each end. Chill for a couple of hours in the fridge then steam the roulade over a pan of boiling water, in the cling film, for about 5 minutes.

Melt the butter in a pan and add the mange tout, new potatoes and garlic and stir-fry until heated through but still crispy.

Make the hollandaise sauce by mixing the egg yolks and vinegar in the food processor, then slowly add the butter and seasoning.

Place stir-fried vegetables on each dinner plate, top with a piece of roulade and serve with the hollandaise sauce.